Pop Showcase for Strings

For Solo or String Orchestra
arranged by JACK BULLOCK

CONTENTS

Project Manager: Thom Proctor
Art Design: Thais Yanes
CD MIDI Sequencing: Chris Lobdell

WARNER BROS. PUBLICATIONS
Warner Music Group
An AOL Time Warner Company
USA: 15800 NW 48th Avenue, Miami, FL 33014

WARNER/CHAPPELL MUSIC
CANADA: 15800 N.W. 48th AVENUE
MIAMI, FLORIDA 33014
SCANDINAVIA: P.O. BOX 533, VENDEVAGEN 85 B
S-182 15, DANDERYD, SWEDEN
AUSTRALIA: P.O. BOX 353
3 TALAVERA ROAD, NORTH RYDE N.S.W. 2113
ASIA: THE PENINSULA OFFICE TOWER, 12th FLOOR
18 MIDDLE ROAD
TSIM SHA TSUI, KOWLOON, HONG KONG

NUOVA CARISCH
ITALY: VIA CAMPANIA, 12
20098 S. GIULIANO MILANESE (MI)
ZONA INDUSTRIALE SESTO ULTERIANO
SPAIN: MAGALLANES, 25
28015 MADRID
FRANCE: CARISCH MUSICOM,
25, RUE D'HAUTEVILLE, 75010 PARIS

IMP
INTERNATIONAL MUSIC PUBLICATIONS LIMITED
ENGLAND: GRIFFIN HOUSE,
161 HAMMERSMITH ROAD, LONDON W6 8BS
GERMANY: MARSTALLSTR. 8, D-80539 MUNCHEN
DENMARK: DANMUSIK, VOGNMAGERGADE 7
DK 1120 KOBENHAVNK

AUGIE'S GREAT MUNICIPAL BAND

Solo Arrangement

By **JOHN WILLIAMS**

String Orchestra Arrangement

EYE OF THE TIGER

Solo Arrangement

String Orchestra Arrangement

Moderate rock ♩ = 104

BLUE TANGO

Solo Arrangement

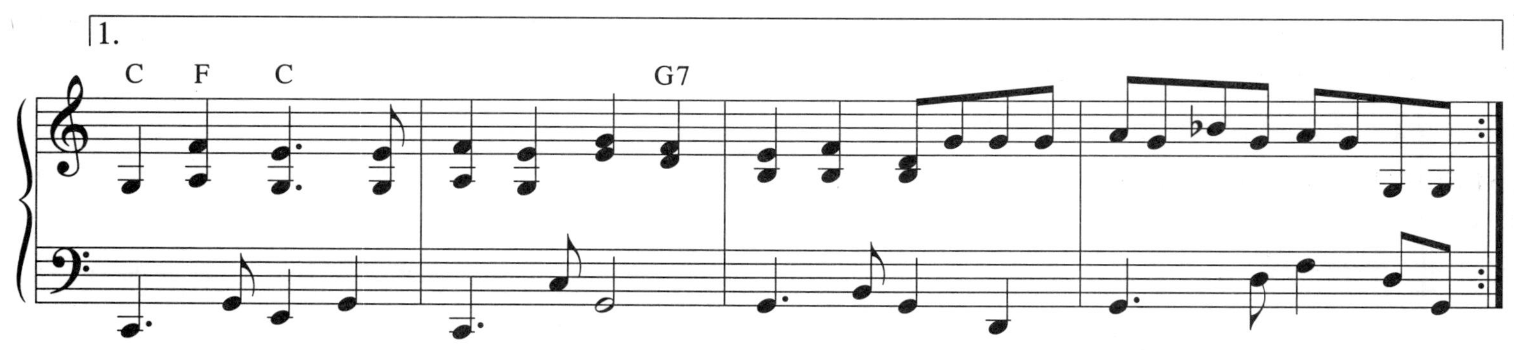

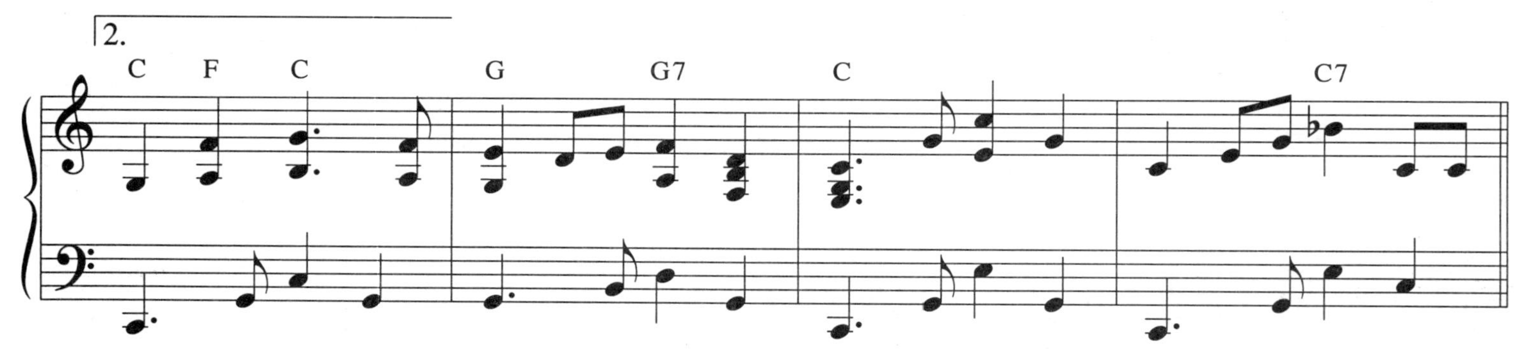

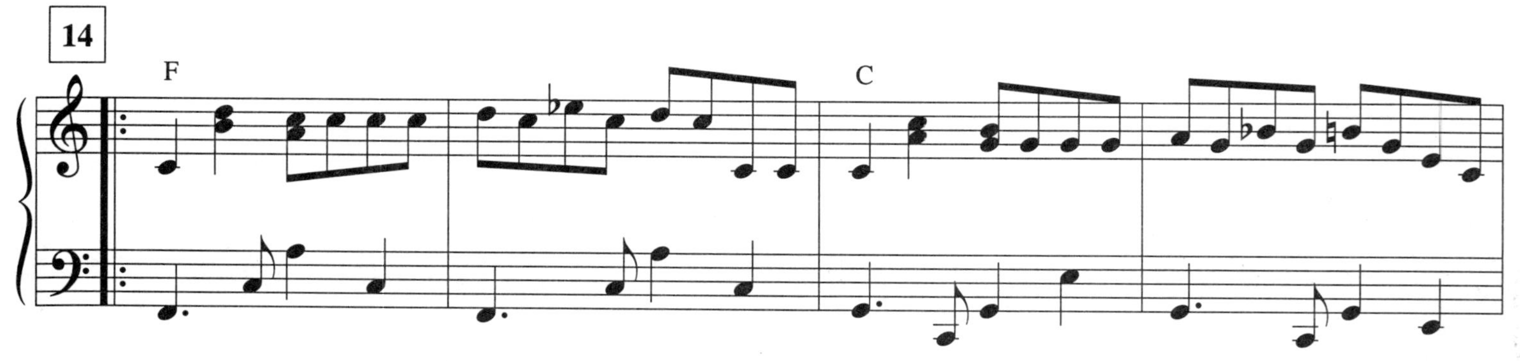

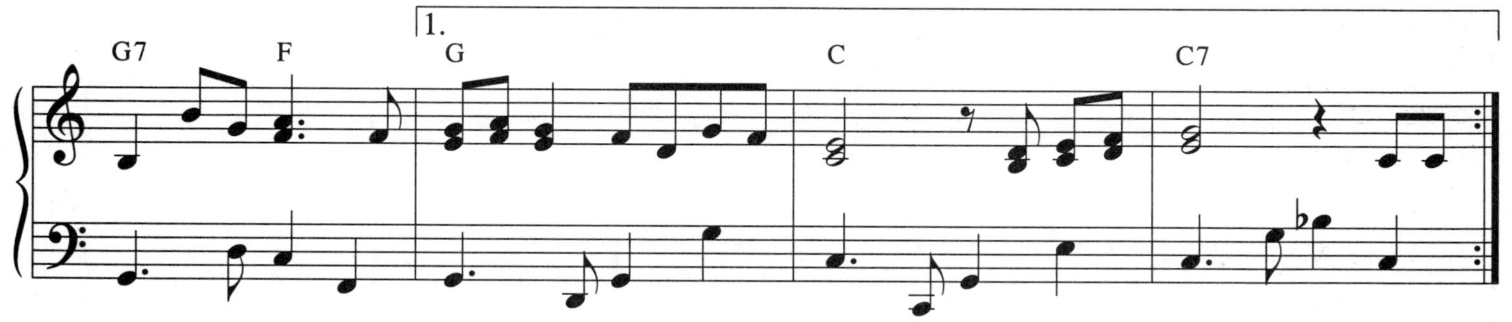

String Orchestra Arrangement

Moderately ♩ = 108

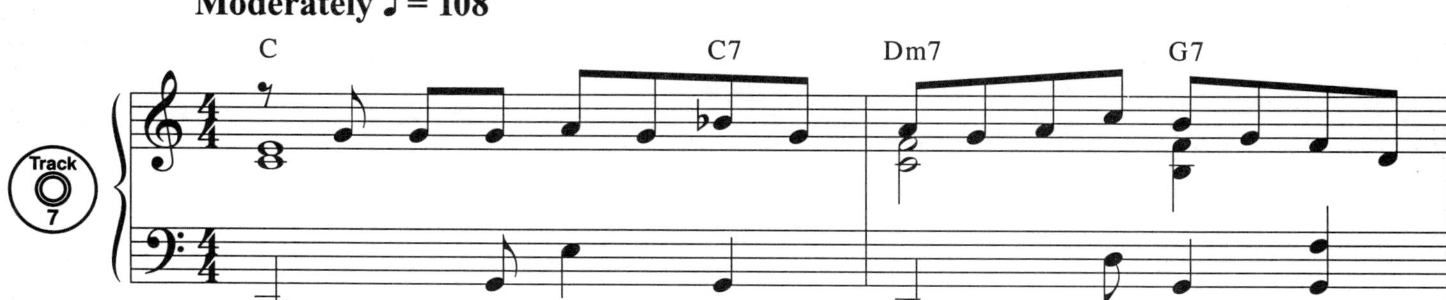

8

1.
C   F   C
G7
2.
C
G7
C
C7
B
F
C
1.
G7   F
G
G7
C
C7
2.
G7
C
G7
C
0598B

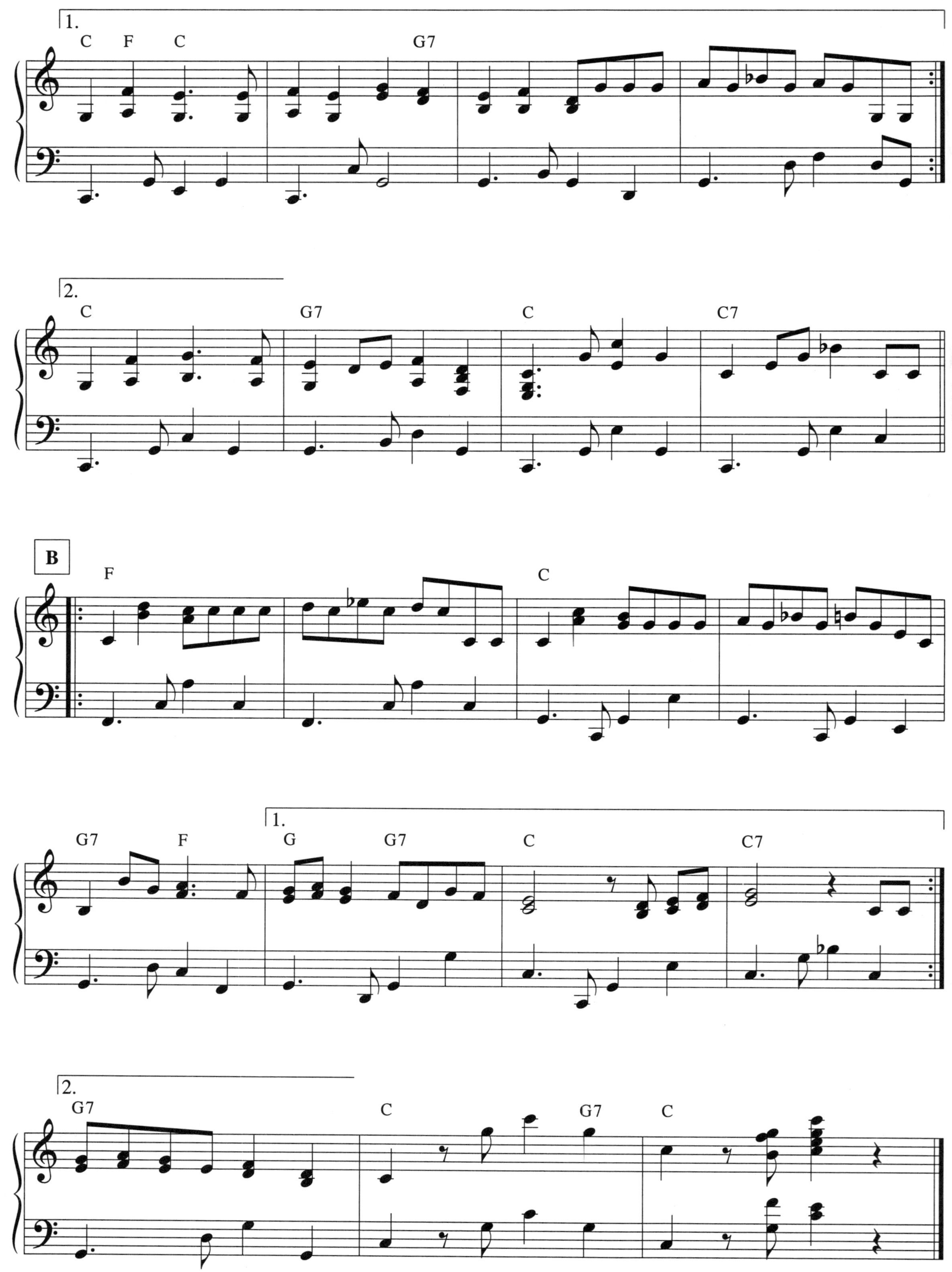

ALL I WANT FOR CHRISTMAS
(Is My Two Front Teeth)

String Orchestra Arrangement

THEME FROM ICE CASTLES
(Through the Eyes of Love)

Solo Arrangement

Music by MARVIN HAMLISCH
Lyrics by CAROLE BAYER SAGER

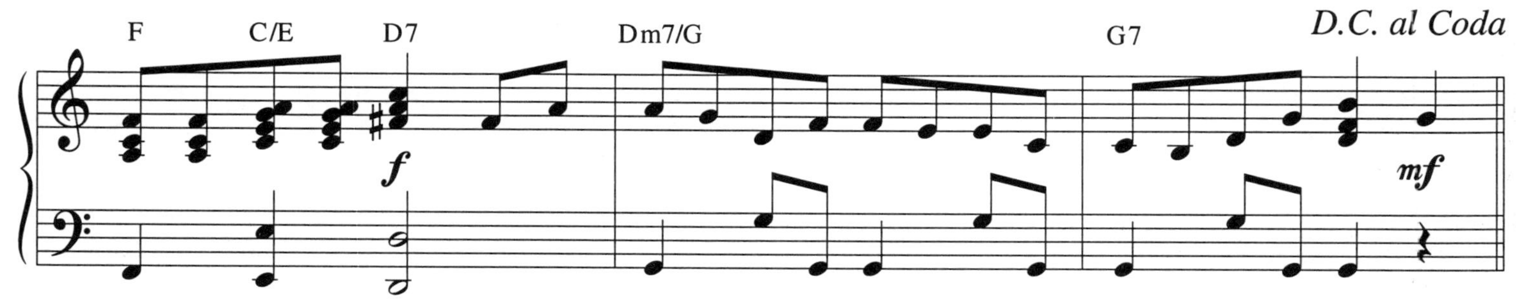

String Orchestra Arrangement

Moderately slow ♩ = 80

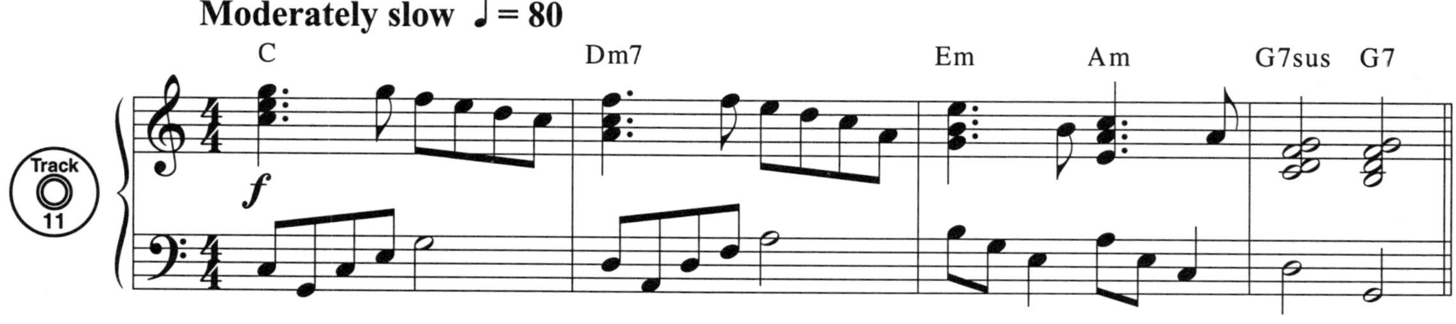

To Coda
Em7   Am7   Fmaj7   E7sus   E7   Am7   Am7/G   D9/F#
f
1.   Dm7/G   G   G7   2.   C   Am   Em7   Am   B
Dm7
f
Em7   Dm7   Dm7/G   C   Dm7   Em7
mf
F   C/E   D7   Dm7/G   G7   D.S. % al Coda
f   mf
Coda
Dm7   G7sus   C
f

(MEET) THE FLINTSTONES

Solo Arrangement

Words and Music by
JOSEPH BARBERA, WILLIAM HANNA
and HOYT CURTIN

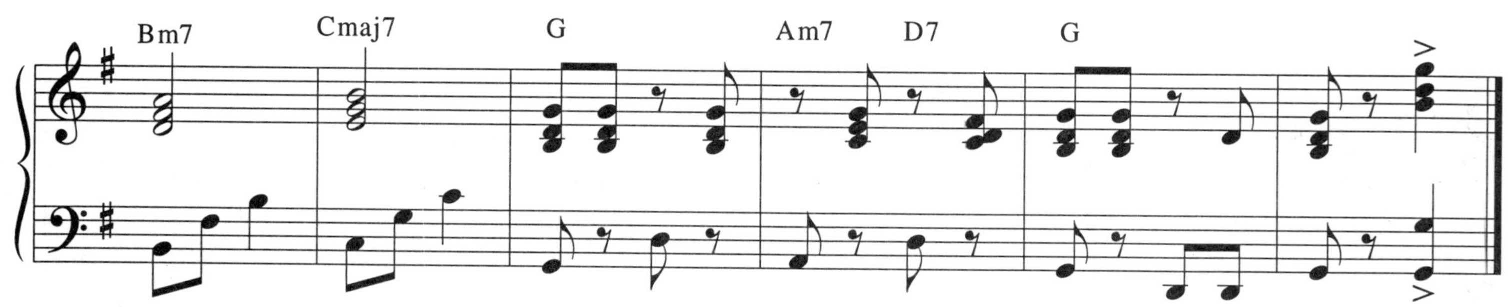

String Orchestra Arrangement

Moderately fast ♩ = 126

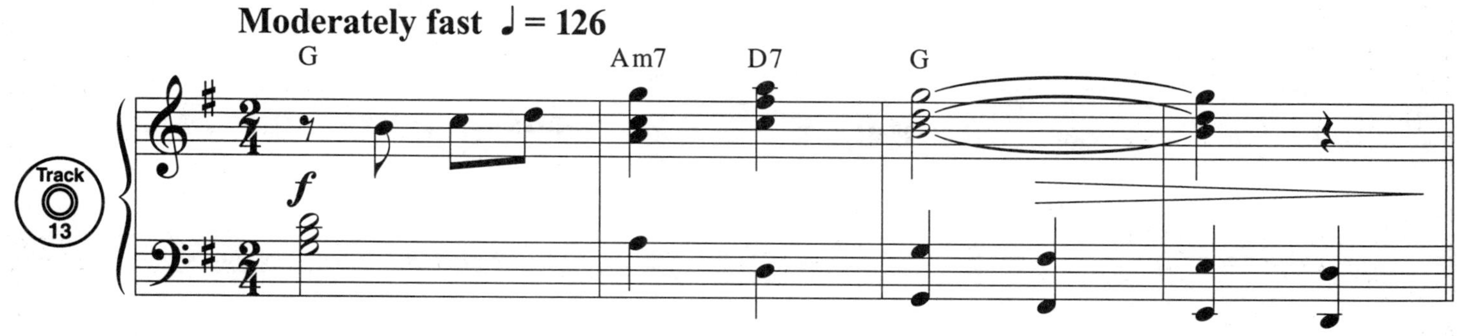

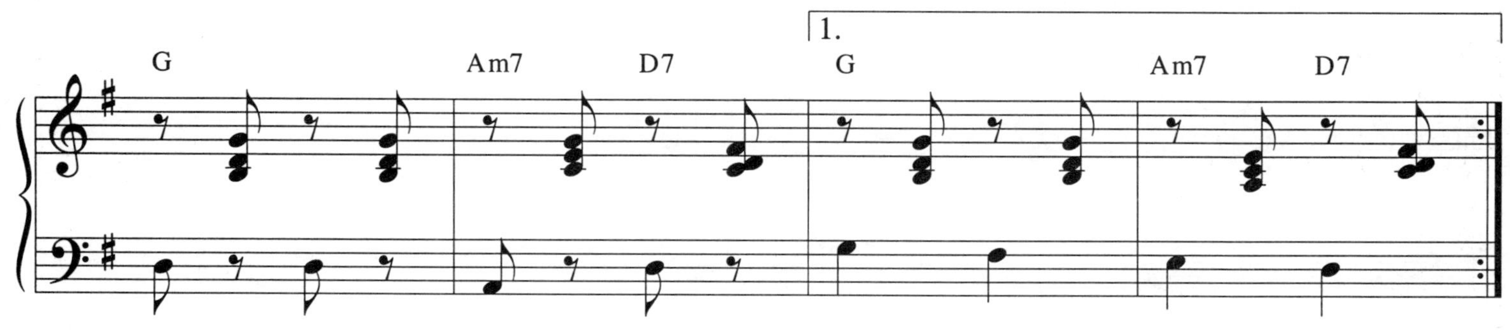

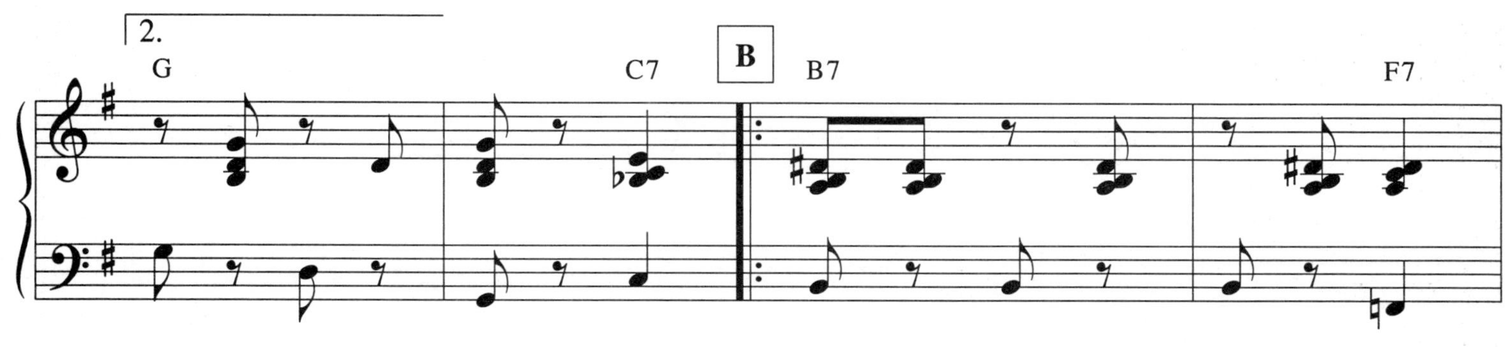

0598B

C
D7
Ab7
G
Am7
Bm7
Cmaj7
G
Am7
D7
G
C7
1.
2.
Am7
Ab7
G
Bb7
Am7
Ab7
G
Bb7
Am7
D7
G
ff

THE ROSE

Words and Music by
AMANDA McBROOM

Solo Arrangement

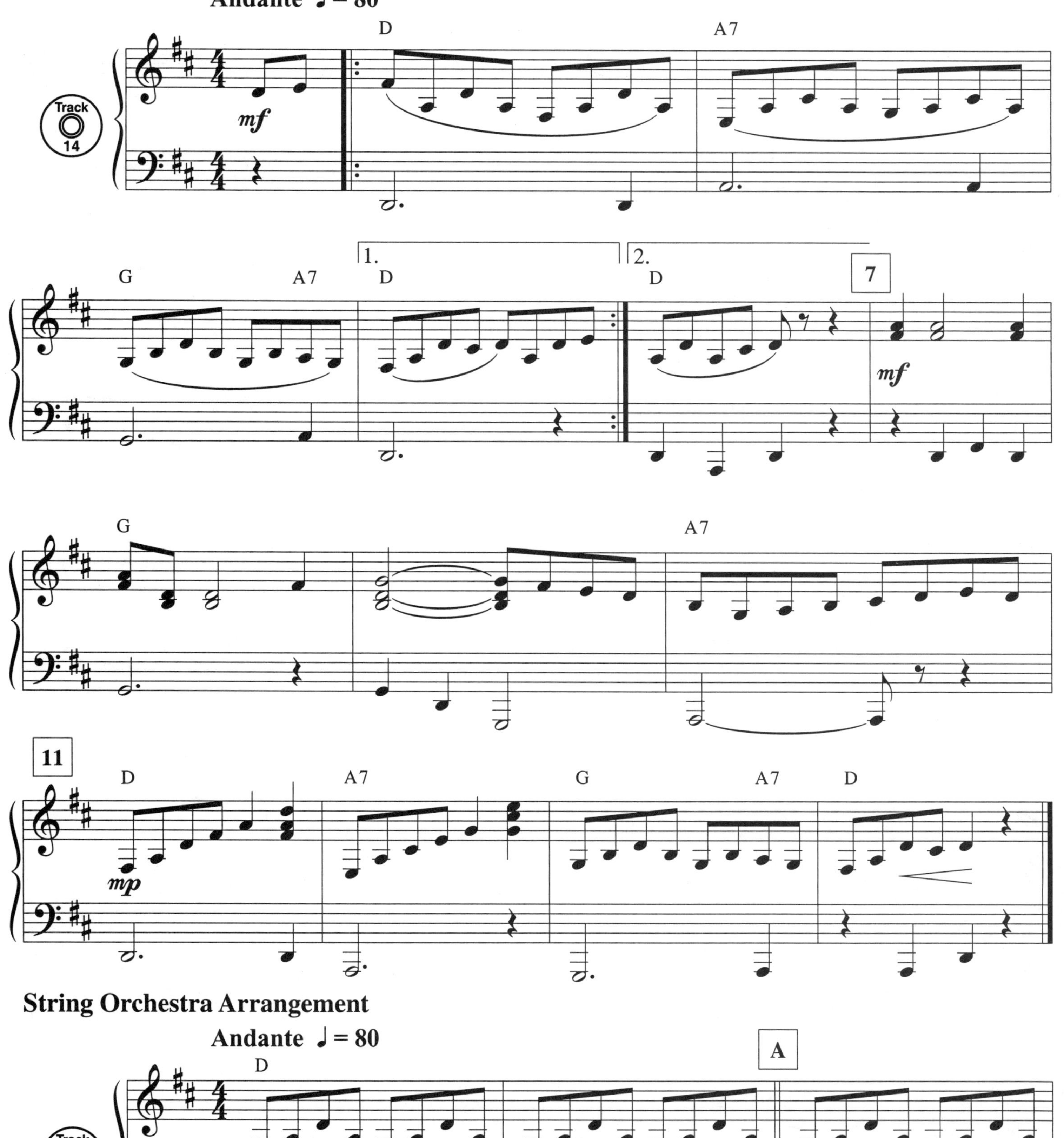

String Orchestra Arrangement

A7
G
A7
D
B
A7
G
A7
D
C
G
A7
mf
D
A7
G
A7
D
mp
E
G
D A7 Bm
G A7
F
D
mf
ritard.
mp
A7
G
A7
D
mf
ritard.

THIS IS IT!

Solo Arrangement

Words and Music by
MACK DAVID and
JERRY LIVINGSTON

0598B

String Orchestra Arrangement

I'M WALKIN'

Solo Arrangement

Words and Music by
ANTOINE DOMINO and
DAVE BARTHOLOMEW

String Orchestra Arrangement

MERRILY WE ROLL ALONG

Solo Arrangement

0598B

String Orchestra Arrangement

Moderato ♩ = 120

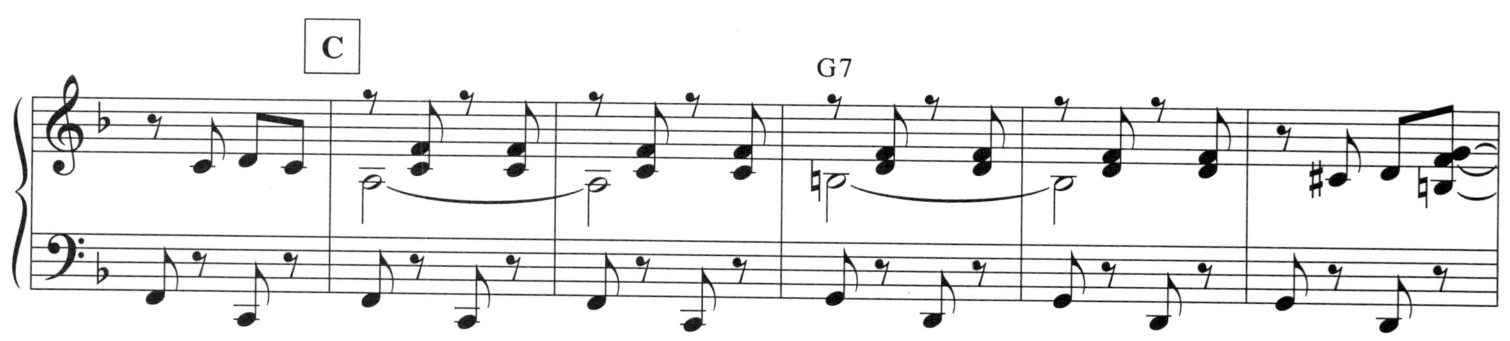

ANIMANIACS
(Main Title)

Lyrics by TOM RUEGER
Music by RICHARD STONE

Solo Arrangement

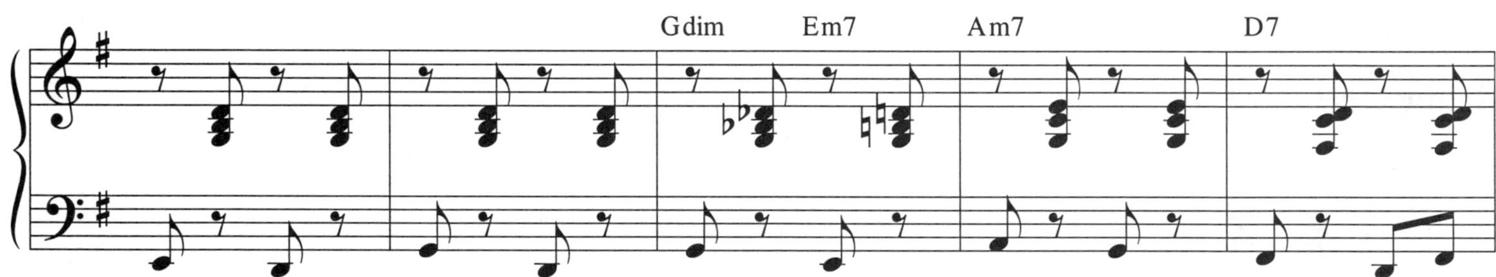

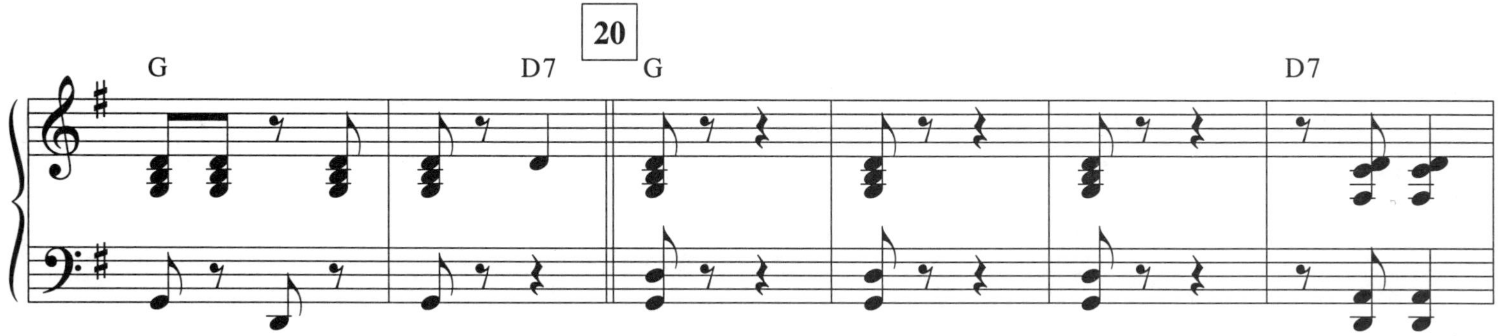

0598B

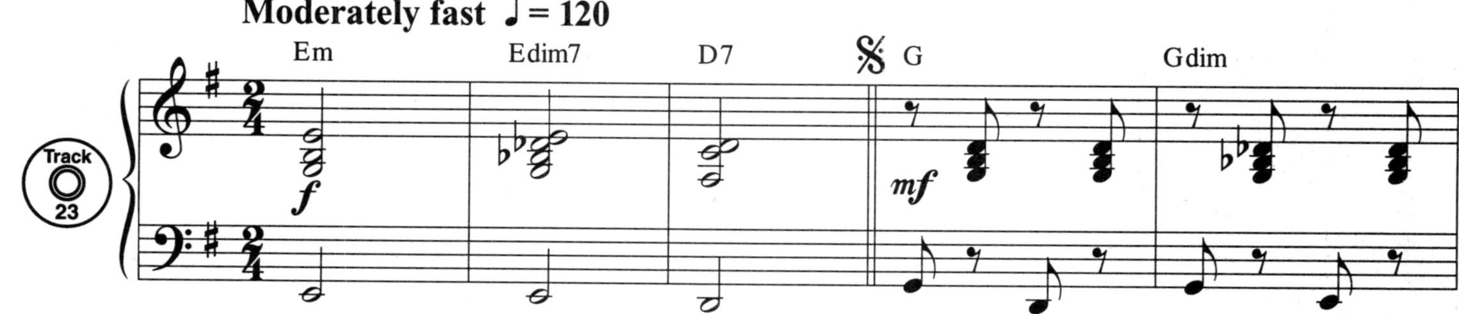

String Orchestra Arrangement

Moderately fast ♩ = 120

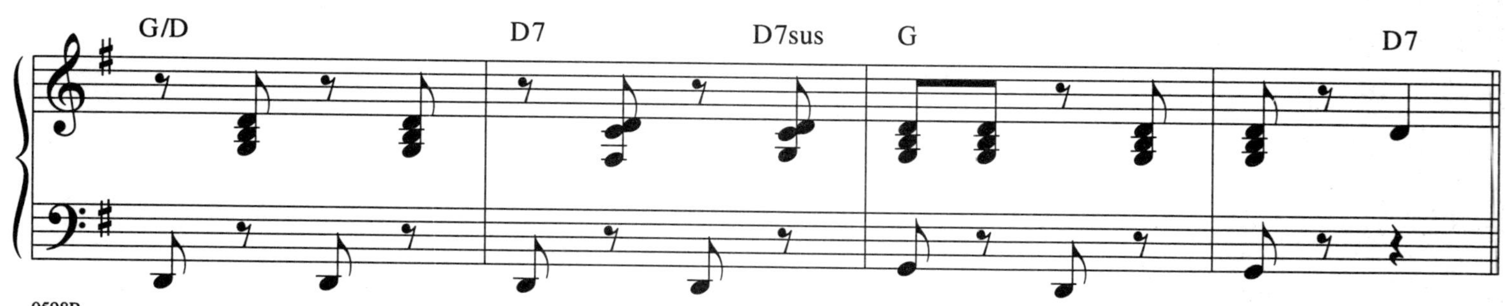

27
B
G
D7
G
C
G7
C
G
Am7
G
A♭dim7
Am7
E♭9
D7
D.S. ⅜ al Coda
Coda
C#dim7
Am7
A7(#5)
D7
Am7
A7(#5)
D7
Am7
A7(#5)
D7
Am7
A7(#5)
D7
G
ff
0598B

STAR WARS
(Main Title)

By JOHN WILLIAMS

Solo Arrangement

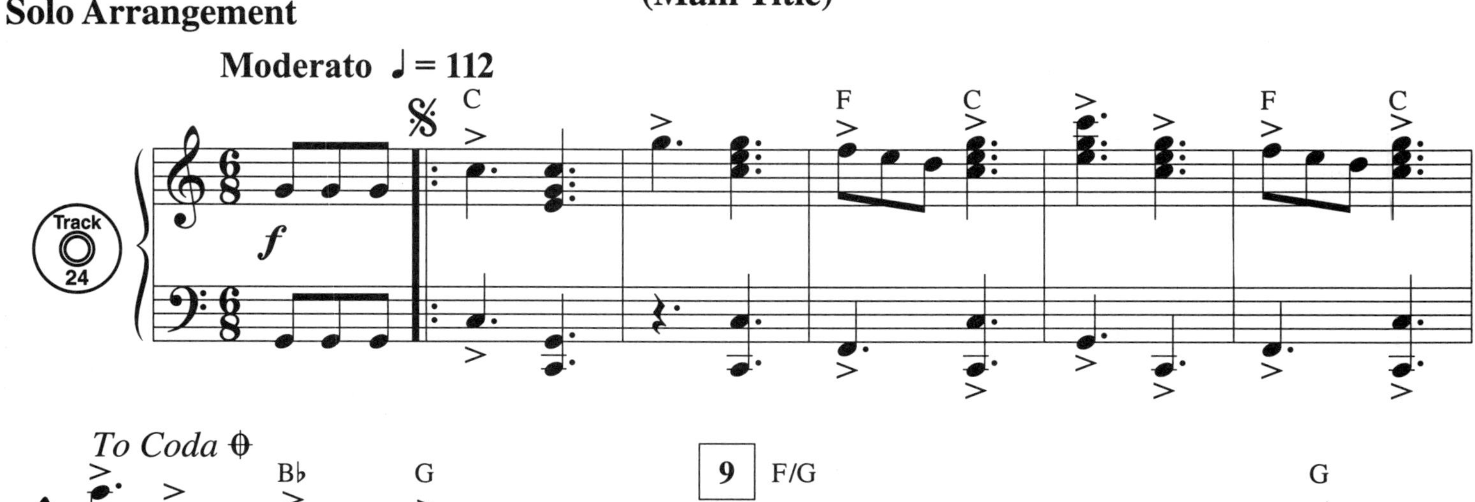

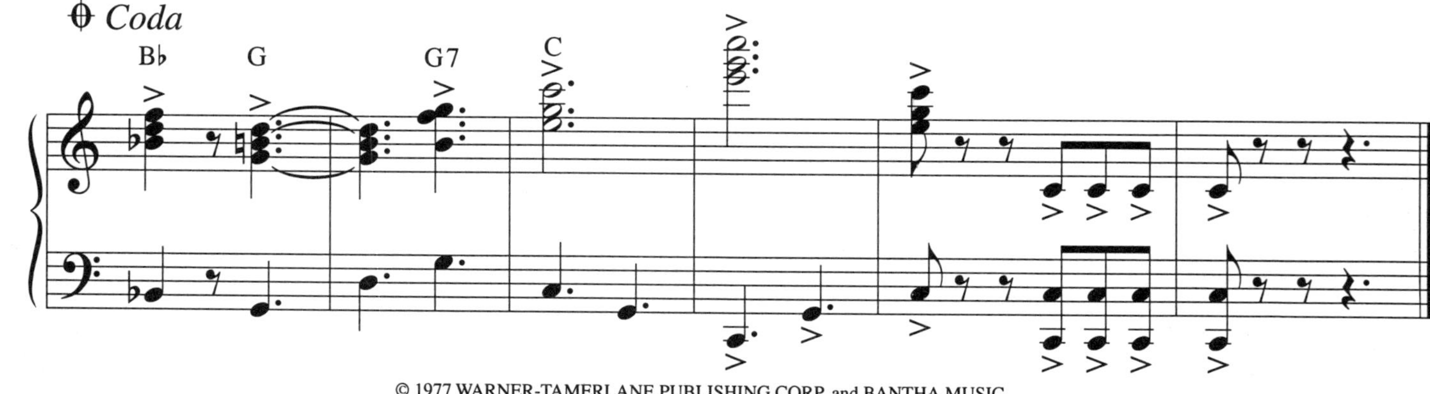

String Orchestra Arrangement

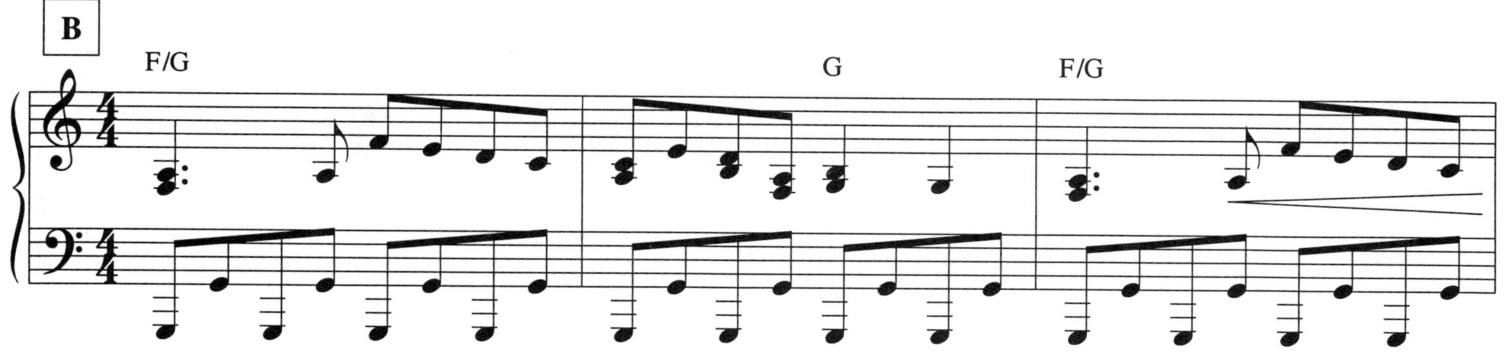

0598B

C
D
E
F
Coda
D.S. al Coda
(with repeat)

THEME FROM SUPERMAN

By **JOHN WILLIAMS**

Solo Arrangement

0598B

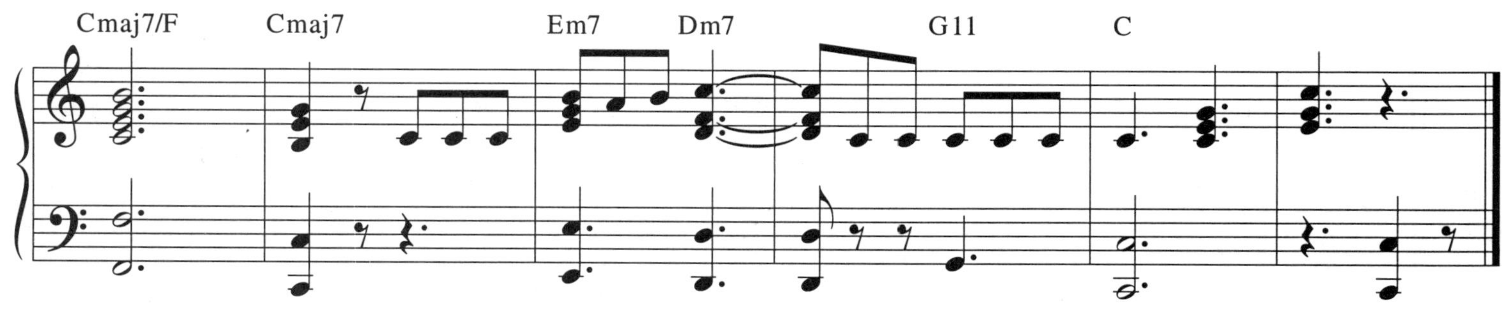

String Orchestra Arrangement

Moderato ♩ = 108